MY FIRST SCIENCE TEXTBOOK

Electron

Los electrones

Written by Mary Wissinger
Illustrated by Harriet Kim Anh Rodis

Created and edited by John J. Coveyou

Science, Naturally!
An imprint of Platypus Media, LLC
Washington, D.C.

I'm negatively charged
and have very little mass.

Mi carga es negativa y
no tengo casi masa.

I'm attracted to the proton.
I'm almost 2,000 times
smaller than it.

Me atrae mucho el protón.
Soy 2,000 veces menor que él.

More electrons could fit on this dot than there are people on the planet.

En este punto caben más electrones que personas en la Tierra ves.

Population–7.7 Billion
Población–7700 millones

I speed far from the nucleus quite unpredictably.

De manera impredecible, lejos del núcleo me muevo.

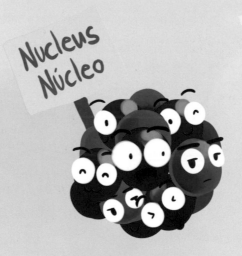

I mostly fly around in a
cloud of probability.

*En una nube de probabilidades,
alrededor de él veloz vuelo.*

Pick which you'd like to calculate—
my speed or my location.

*Elige si calcular mi velocidad
o mi posición.*

You can't know both at once.
It's an uncertain situation.

Es imposible saber ambas.
Qué misteriosa situación.

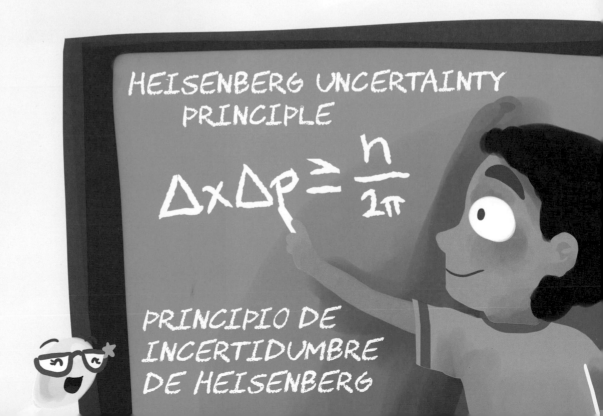

Look around this room;
see anything that's glowing?

Observa esta habitación.
¿Ves algo que resplandece?

If it's powered by electricity, that means electrons are flowing.

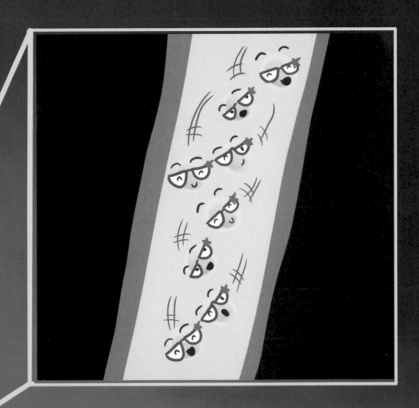

Si la electricidad lo alimenta, es un flujo de electrones que aparece.

When it's cold and dry in winter, electrons build up when you walk.

Cuando caminas en el invierno frío y seco, los electrones acumularás.

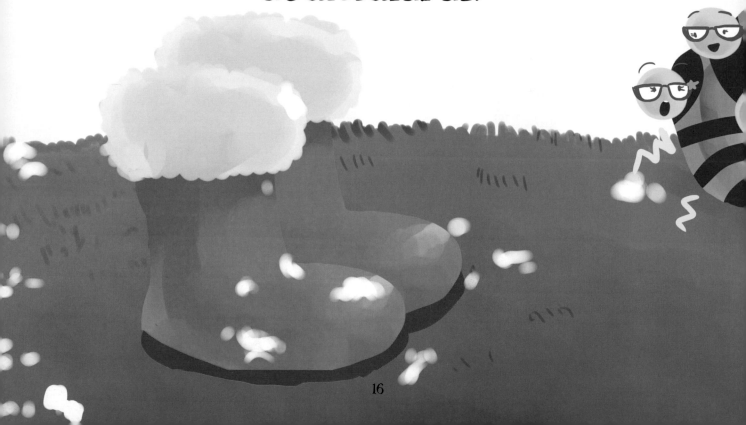

16

Touch something and I'll jump to balance out.

Si tocas algo, yo saltaré para equilibrar la carga.

18

You'll feel a
static shock.

Y un *choque*
estático **sentirás.**

Electrons are mysterious,
and we change how we behave.

*Los electrones somos misteriosos
y nuestro comportamiento
suele cambiar.*

Watch close and we act like particles.

Si nos observas de cerca
somos partículas.

Observed / Observado

Double Slit Experiment /
Experimento de doble rendija

22

Turn your back
and we act like waves.

Actuamos como ondas si la espalda nos das.

23

Double Slit Experiment / Experimento de doble rendija

Unobserved / No observado

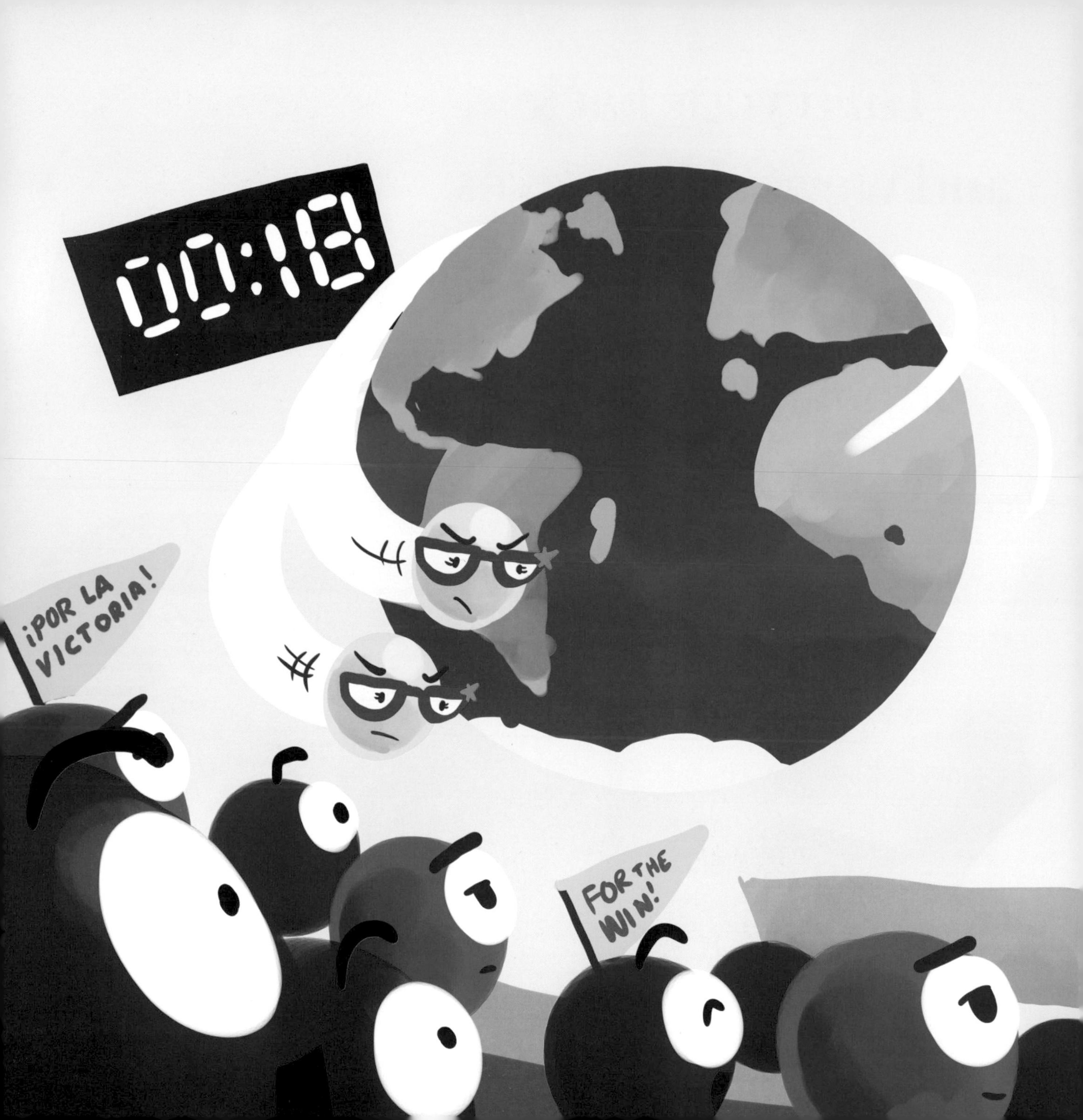
00:18
¡POR LA VICTORIA!
FOR THE WIN!

If we were in a race, we could circle the world in eighteen seconds.

Podemos dar la vuelta al mundo en dieciocho segundos. ¡Zas!

Electrons are a part of the atom, but we are subatomic legends!

¡Los **electrones** somos una parte del átomo, pero somos leyendas subatómicas!

Glossary

ATOMS: The building blocks for all matter in our universe. They are so small that you can't see them, and are made up of even smaller particles called protons, neutrons, and electrons.

DOUBLE SLIT EXPERIMENT: A demonstration showing that electrons can act like both waves and particles at the same time—a concept known as wave-particle duality.

CHARGE: An electric charge is a property of matter. There are two types of electric charges: positive and negative. Protons have a positive charge and electrons have a negative charge.

ELECTRICITY: A type of energy created when electrons move from one atom to another in the same direction. Electricity is the flow of electrons.

ELECTRONS: Very teeny particles with a negative electric charge. Electrons travel around the nucleus of every atom.

HEISENBERG UNCERTAINTY PRINCIPLE: A rule discovered by physicist Werner Heisenberg, which tells us that the location and the speed of a particle, like an electron, can't be measured at the same time.

MASS: A measure of how much matter is in an object. Mass is different from weight because the mass of an object never changes, but its weight will change based on its location in the universe.

NEUTRONS: Very teeny particles with no electric charge, found in the nucleus of most atoms.

NUCLEUS: The center of an atom, made up of protons and neutrons.

PARTICLES: Tiny, singular bits of matter that can range in size from subatomic particles, such as electrons, to ones large enough to be seen, such as particles of dust floating in sunlight.

PROBABILITY: Probability is the likelihood that something will happen. It is impossible to know exactly where an electron will be inside an atom, because electrons are always moving very fast, but scientists can calculate the probability of an electron being in a certain area. An atomic orbital, or electron cloud (pictured as the ring around the nucleus), is the part of an atom where an electron is likely to be.

PROTONS: Very teeny particles with a positive electric charge. Protons are in the nucleus of every atom.

STATIC SHOCK: When an object or person has a negative charge from extra electrons, and they touch an object that has a positive charge from too few electrons, electricity jumps between the two. You might feel a static shock when you touch something made of metal.

SUBATOMIC PARTICLE: A particle that is smaller than an atom and exists within it, like protons, neutrons, or electrons.

WAVES: A repeated up-and-down pattern of movement that lets energy travel from one place to another. Sound waves, light waves, and ocean waves are examples of different types of waves.

Glosario

ÁTOMOS: Son los bloques de construcción de toda la materia que existe en el universo. Son tan pequeños que no se pueden ver y están hechos de partículas más pequeñas llamadas protones, neutrones y electrones.

CARGA ELÉCTRICA: Los protones tienen una carga positiva y los electrones una carga negativa. Como los extremos positivo y negativo de un imán, las cargas opuestas se atraen.

CHOQUE ESTÁTICO: Cuando un objeto o una persona tiene carga negativa por haber acumulado electrones, y toca un objeto que tiene una carga positiva porque ha perdido electrones, la electricidad salta entre los dos. Puedes sentir un choque estático cuando tocas algo metálico.

ELECTRICIDAD: Un tipo de energía que se crea cuando los electrones se mueven de un átomo a otro en la misma dirección. La electricidad es el flujo de electrones.

ELECTRONES: Partículas muy pequeñas con una carga eléctrica negativa. Los electrones viajan alrededor del núcleo de cada átomo.

EXPERIMENTO DE DOBLE RENDIJA: Es un experimento que muestra que los electrones pueden actuar como ondas y partículas al mismo tiempo, un concepto conocido como la dualidad onda-partícula.

MASA: Es la medida de cuánta materia tiene un objeto. La masa es diferente del peso porque la masa de un objeto nunca cambia, pero el peso puede cambiar dependiendo en dónde esté el objeto en el espacio.

NEUTRONES: Partículas muy pequeñas sin ninguna carga eléctrica, que se encuentran en el núcleo de casi todos los átomos.

NÚCLEO: El centro de un átomo, compuesto de protones y neutrones.

ONDAS: Un patrón repetido de movimiento hacia arriba y hacia abajo que transfiere energía de un lugar a otro. Las ondas de sonido, las ondas de luz y las ondas del mar son ejemplos de tipo de ondas.

PARTÍCULAS: Diminutos pedacitos de masa que pueden oscilar en tamaño desde partículas subatómicas, como los electrones, hasta partículas más grandes que se pueden ver a simple vista, como motas de polvo que se ven a la luz del sol.

PARTÍCULA SUBATÓMICA: Una partícula que es más pequeña que un átomo y existe dentro de él, como los protones, los neutrones y los electrones.

PRINCIPIO DE INCERTIDUMBRE DE HEISENBERG: La posición y la velocidad de una partícula no pueden medirse con precisión al mismo tiempo.

PROBABILIDAD: Es el cálculo de la posibilidad de que algo ocurra. Es imposible saber exactamente dónde estará un electrón dentro de un átomo, porque los electrones siempre se mueven muy rápido, pero los científicos pueden calcular la probabilidad de que un electrón esté en una zona determinada. Un orbital atómico, o nube de electrones (representada como el anillo que rodea el núcleo), es la parte de un átomo donde es probable que esté un electrón.

PROTONES: Partículas muy pequeñas con una carga eléctrica positiva. Los protones están en el núcleo de cada átomo.

"To my parents, who taught me to love books."
"A mis padres, que me enseñaron a amar los libros."

—Harriet Kim Anh Rodis

My First Science Textbook: Electrons / Los electrones
Copyright © 2021, 2016 Genius Games, LLC
Originally published by Genius Games, LLC in 2016

Written by Mary Wissinger
Illustrated by Harriet Kim Anh Rodis with Uzuri Designs
Created and edited by John J. Coveyou
Translated by Michelle A. Ramirez
Spanish-language consultants: Eida de la Vega and Andrea Batista

Published by Science, Naturally!
Bilingual (En/Sp) paperback first edition • September 2021 • ISBN: 978-1-938492-49-5
Bilingual (En/Sp) eBook first edition • September 2021 • ISBN: 978-1-938492-50-1
English hardback first edition • 2016 • ISBN: 978-1-945779-01-5
     Second edition • June 2021
English paperback first edition • September 2021 • ISBN: 978-1-938492-48-8
English eBook first edition • 2016 • ISBN: 978-1-945779-07-7
English board book first edition • 2016 • ISBN: 978-1-945779-04-6

Enjoy all the titles in the series:
     Atoms • Los átomos
     Protons and Neutrons • Los protones y los neutrones
     Electrons • Los electrones

Teacher's Guide available at the Educational Resources page of ScienceNaturally.com.

Published in the United States by:
     Science, Naturally!
          An imprint of Platypus Media, LLC
     725 8th Street, SE, Washington, D.C. 20003
     202-465-4798 • Fax: 202-558-2132
     Info@ScienceNaturally.com • ScienceNaturally.com

Distributed to the trade by:
     National Book Network (North America)
          301-459-3366 • Toll-free: 800-462-6420
          CustomerCare@NBNbooks.com • NBNbooks.com
     NBN international (worldwide)
          NBNi.Cservs@IngramContent.com • Distribution.NBNi.co.uk

Library of Congress Control Number: 2021937181

10 9 8 7 6 5 4 3 2 1

Printed in Canada